WINDSWEPT LEAVES

NEW AND SELECTED HAIKU

LUKE LEVI

YELLOW LEAF PRESS

ACKNOWLEDGEMENTS

Some of the haiku poems were first published in the following places: *Akitsu Quarterly, Autumn Moon Haiku Journal, Cold Moon Journal, Failed Haiku, Fireflies' Light, Five Fleas (Itchy Poetry), Haiku in Action (Nick Virgilio Haiku Association), Haiku Commentary, Humana Obscura, Japan Society, LitStream Magazine, Narrative Northeast, Poetry Pea, The Tide Rises, The Tide Falls, The Wee Sparrow Poetry Press, Trash Panda, Vagus,* and *Wales Haiku Journal.*

WHAT IS HAIKU?

Due to many debating on what haiku is, it's necessary to first explain a short history of the haiku poem.

Haiku first started in 13th century Japan. A short introductory poem to the renga poem was called hokku. A renga was a hundred stanzas long that was composed syllabically and spoken orally. The renga was composed collaboratively but a hokku was written by a single person.

In the 17th century, Bashō, his birth name Matsuo Kinsaku (1644-1694), began to write hokku but without a long renga poem after it.

This hokku poem is now called haiku. However, if Japanese haiku were translated strictly into English, it'd be a single line poem, called monoku, which some haiku writers today choose to follow in form. It took around 300 years for the hokku to branch off from the long renga poem.

About 300 years later, haiku poetry still retains its

essence. With its beginning in 13th century Japan, this nearly 400-year-old poetry form is unusual for lasting this long in popularity.

Although, since early 1900s, the haiku has slightly changed. In many haiku magazines today, many prominent haiku writers do not follow a 5-7-5 syllabic pattern.

Although we are mistakenly taught in school that the form is 5-7-5 in syllables, this is a myth. The original Japanese haiku writers counted sounds in the form of *on*, not syllables.

This means that 12 *syllables* is equal to 17 *on*. The word haiku counts as two syllables but three *on* (ha-i-ku), even though you don't say it that way.

However, English-speaking haiku writers over the centuries do keep the essence of the poem. A haiku typically involves the following:

- depicts an image
- written in present tense
- composed in three lines
- uses simple language
- uses a 'cutting word' that 'cuts' the poem in two parts
- references a season ('kigo' is a seasonal word or phrase)
- 17 syllables or less

Also, succinctness is more important than strict

syllabic form. You will find that haiku masters sometimes deviated from strict form.

In the below poem, Bashō is following the traditional 5-7-5 *on* (in its original Japanese poem), yet the poem is eight syllables in the English translation:

fu-ru-i-ke ya (5)
ka-wa-zu to-bi-ko-mu (7)
mi-zu-no-o-to (5)

old pond (2)
frog leaps in (3)
water's sound (3)

It's difficult to translate poems correctly; some may say it's impossible. In my writing, I try to keep the essence of the haiku alive, since counting syllables becomes a bit silly after doing it for thousands of poems.

Besides Bashō, other masters of haiku are Yosa Buson (1716–1784), Masaoka Shiki (1867-1902) and Kobayashi Issa (1763–1828). Along with Bashō, these are the four major haiku poets that are still studied today.

It's not the words that matter the most but the feeling and image they evoke in the reader. Even with simple language, haiku can be powerful poetry. Like the best poetry, if it's written from the heart, the effect will be strong.

— Luke Levi

the world is absurd
but I still cling to its flowers
like a bee drunk on spring

full moon
even the flowers
shine white

we listen
to songbirds
the fly and I

sky dance
above the cedar trees
two dragonflies

it is so soft a thing
moonlit raindrop
rushes down the window

this cricket
keeping me awake
how sweet its song

liquid gold—
the sunset melts
into a pond

even in paradise
one desires home
like a migrating bird

gentle taps on the roof
then a roaring of rain
falling together

a deer's shadow
stretches far
from moonlight

knowing nothing
of worldly things
a butterfly is born

hope lives
on a spiderweb
shivering in a rainstorm

on the drive home
the stars hang low
almost touching the hills

the dog is silent
but its bark still echoes
from the cedar valley

in the silence
of an unfolding flower
a bee finds home

soft as a kiss
rain patting
the window

dark clouds
tease rain
but only sunlight falls

once the heart is lost
it's free to fly anywhere
like this hooting owl

rock bottom—
river stones form
gentle waves

as if with love
the peach tree lets fall
a wrinkled leaf

we're back from death
the wildflowers and I
in the peace of spring

this lake
collects memories
as floating leaves

everyone
is asleep but me...
my eyes long for stars

a finch calls—
the laughing coyote
answers

showered in moonlight
in want of love
the owl hoots

loneliness
like a storm
it comes and goes

tiny frog
you also are covered
in morning dew

like a fallen leaf
I also will become
the earth

to sing of rain
is to love wildflowers
sprouting from mud

the moon is so close
I cradle it in my palms
like a white fruit

to fly
the caterpillar
must let go of its old self

so fragile
are the beautiful things
withered flowers

by falling down
I see the wildflowers
much better

migrating birds—
every tree
looks like home

the red sunset
welcomes early-rising bats
in droves

like wrinkles
only the foam is left
of the sea

even now
hope remains
as a seed in the soil

this bending tree
in a thousand years
will touch the pond

near songbirds
the troubles of this world
disappear like morning fog

my shadow waits for me
as I stop to look
at the flowers

awoken first by sunlight
then by songbirds...
spring rising

above my grave
I hope a nearby tree
houses songbirds

today is like the silence
between each poem
a calm interlude

a comforting sound:
rain falling down the window
making the eyes tired

autumn—
rain on ice-lined windows
like dripping candle wax

field of sleeping grass
is copper in the waning light
of winter

the sky
like yesterday
getting brighter

alive for centuries
this oak tree
turns yellow again

orange butterfly
following me
you know I seek flowers too

early spring—
oak trees budding
yellow as the sun

caught
between two worlds
an owl at sunset

what loses luster
may return with color
like awakening wildflowers

the bee
flying into flowers
intoxicated by spring

a ladybug
mistakes me
for a flower

a bare tree—
three cardinals
replace the leaves

cotton-white cloud
soaring across the sky,
how far have you travelled?

what died
appears to return
grass sprouts

morning sun
an echoing birdsong
full of love

step carefully on earth—
that ant carries a crumb
of cheese to his family

we go anywhere
the wind will take us
floating butterfly

morning rain
on dusty windows:
a view of green hills

mountainside
a row of sheep
ends in fog

the cool winds
she promised
goosebumps

Halloween—
pretending
to be dead

changing size
up and down green hills
a vulture's shadow

flash flood
the spider
webs a new home

windy spring
the house painter
watches color fly

little bee
how far will you
buzz today?

while it lasts
a white butterfly
clings to the daffodil

how soft the light
it falls through green veins
of leaves

one yellow leaf
of a bare tree
hangs onto the past

invisible as night rain
my future anchors
in the bed of dreams

December—
cedar pollen rising
out of the hills like smoke

only one sound
wide black wings flapping
above the live oak

mindlessly
drifting to the flowers
the butterfly and I

how softly
the rain falls
on the oak hills

little cloud of rain
goes it alone
apart from the storm

winter sky—
the colors sing
from songbirds

silence—
a white heron soars
over the cedar hills

picking up fallen leaves
the wind returns them
to my eyes

a short lifespan
the butterfly can't stop hugging
the flowers

my death will be
like a wildflower that returns
in spring

so peaceful
this cold day of gentle rain
singing birds silent

creaking door
listening to spirits
in old walls

where ocean
meets sky
the same shade of blue

the joke ran flat
my strangeness is now akin
to a two-legged dog

end of year
have I changed with the seasons
or am I evergreen?

a finch chants three songs
each one echoes over hills
and ends in the heart

bee
dusted in pollen
flies from the redbud

roadblock
the detour is full
of wildflower hills

how lonely it is to be feared
by cheerful birds—
hawk atop fencepost

after confusing
the window for trees
a finch hops away

blowing wind
passing through oak leaves...
I forget myself

the day is silent
but sunlight keeps on singing
in my heart

rain pats the roof
as if a small animal
is running on it

white stars—
crape myrtle flowers
in her hair

autumn—
an old windmill
cawing with a crow

as a red leaf falls
the world appears well inside
this forest of calm

gazing at new leaves
from the sunny window
sleepy cat

it comes closer
every day to the hills
spring sun

the sunrise
stole my moon away
leaving a sky of gold

like a whisper
gentle wind shakes
the oak leaves

evening calm
a tree shadow
on the pond

after war
flowers rise from graves
and vines climb crumbling ruins

silent night—
a thin cloud passes
through the moon

fluttering butterfly
her heart is not still
not even for a moment

strange world
even a hummingbird
looks unreal

listeners of night
in the thrum of crickets

                    this world of illusions
                    fades to dreams

sun
after rainfall
leaves become diamonds

pale moon
I tell her we'll meet
one day

waxy oak leaves
shine white in the sun
flickering like stars

at the dusk of life
I will float as wind
through a sunflower field

in the ditch of life
nowhere to go but up...
blinking stars

like the rain
she falls on me
unexpectedly

yellow clouds
peel off from the sun
like lemon skin

dog barking
to the full moon—
primordial habit

how easily it goes—
yellow butterfly
in the wind

house finch
calm as the wind-swept cedar
splashes water on its wings

butterfly
you also hurry
to see the last flowers

in a dark place
a bluebonnet rises
from dead leaves

full moon
within the raindrop
falling from a leaf

in the world of concrete
a roadrunner dashes
across the street

white eye of the sun
on mirrored water
a frog dives into summer

October—
bare branches
whining like old doors

this apple tree
bears no fruit
but I love its shade

summer—
a butterfly clings
to its old home

moonlight
on oak leaves
darkness is not so dark

a butterfly
flies off with
the sunset's color

sometimes my life
twists over too
leaf on the grass

alone...
a singing frog
proves me wrong

early autumn
a cold wind passes
through the flowers

air quality alert
the hawk in the clouds
doesn't know

a white pearl
floating on the pond
autumn moon

lightning—
sometimes my heart
is erratic as this storm

heavy fog—
the tree I normally see
is a phantom

like opening flowers
outspread branches
of ice-lined cedar trees

autumn
a bee remains
in summer flowers

charred wings
circle the sun
three vultures

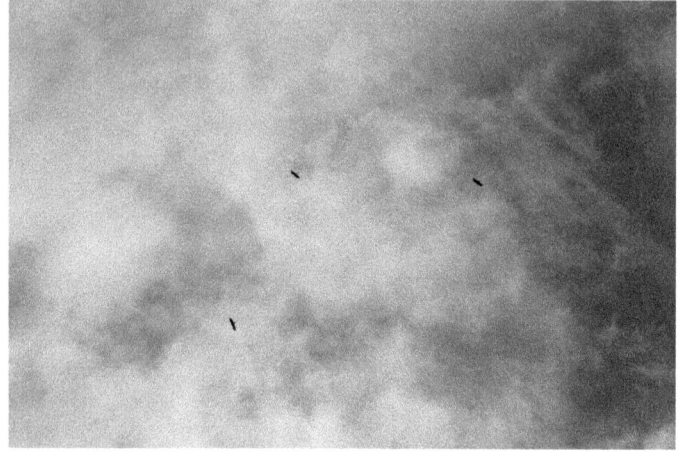

above the trees
rose petals glide
as red butterflies

like us
the butterfly clings to illusions
plastic flower

a coyote
finishes the song
of a fading ambulance

heat wave
in spring
red moon

blissful
watching butterflies
kiss flowers

singing crickets
so loud in summer
their songs play in my dreams

strong scents—
flowers like lovers
I kiss each with my nose

a dark veil
muffles the sun
still its light shines through

gold sunset
the dove coo echoes
from sunflowers

hummingbird
its beak a black sword
piercing the sky

moon songs
from crickets
gazing at stars

so beautifully
does she redden
Japanese maple

it is good news
to hear your trees
are like wildflower hills

walking together
two faces on the pond
the moon and I

like fragments of sun
yellow leaves float
down the green river

a big cloud
crossing the hill country
swallows my shadow

in cool waves
the first winds of autumn
passing through cedar hills

songs in the dark
made mostly of silence
from a hooting owl

coconut palms
blowing one way
before the storm

longhorns
touch the stars
with their horns

on a lonely road
you may find yourself happy
alone at sunset

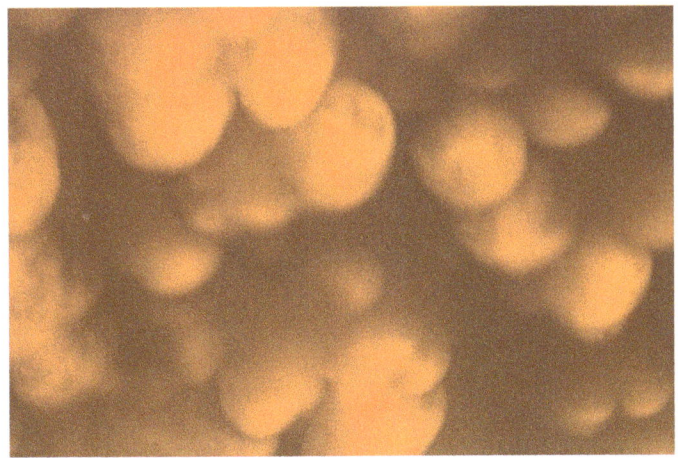

shattering in the water
from a fish tail
autumn moon

swiftly
a finch's shadow
sweeps the grass

dark forest—
from little light
wildflowers

red lanterns
dangling in the jungle
fuchsia flowers

yellow butterfly
do you remember
your past life?

star sleepers—
owl hoots
commence dreams

even the flowers
that took their time
bloom

red flower
petals like velvet
rugs for bugs

following no one
except the wild animals
that made the best path

little bug in my hair
how is the view
up there?

two ducks in a pond
swimming with stars
my soul and hers

like this butterfly
I am passing through
the forests of life

red-leafed tree
the top of it
lost in snow

autumn—
windswept leaves
the calm they give

THANK YOU

Thank you so much for reading my poetry book! It took six months to collect the poems into this book. *Windswept Leaves* collects my most favorite and popular poems from the past five years. So, I'm happy to have shared these poems with you.

If you don't mind, leaving a review would be greatly appreciated. Reviews help new people find my books. Reviews are extremely helpful for an independent writer like myself, and I appreciate each one.

You can leave a review on Goodreads or, if you bought this book from an online store, the store's website, or both.

In the meantime, before my next poetry book comes out in the following years, you can find me on social media sites. You can also email me at: lukelevi4@gmail.com

Instagram @lukelevipoet

TikTok @lukelevipoet

Goodreads: https://www.goodreads.com/lukelevi

Thanks again for reading my book!

ABOUT THE AUTHOR

Luke Levi is a poet and photographer. His poems can be found in more than twenty magazines in the US and UK. Most of his photos depict the Texas Hill Country. You can find him on Instagram @lukelevipoet and learn more about him at lukelevi.com.

facebook.com/lukelevipoet

instagram.com/lukelevipoet

OTHER POETRY BOOKS BY
LUKE LEVI

So Fragile Are the Beautiful Things

Sun

www.ingramcontent.com/pod-product-compliance
Lightning Source LLC
Chambersburg PA
CBHW051329120626
46547CB00016B/2458